TEN L

SPOZ

First published in the United Kingdom in 2017 by ...
Bostin Productions
Birmingham
B45 8QF

Cover design and layout by Spoz

Photographs by Spoz unless otherwise stated. Photographs of Spoz's parents were taken by unknown photographers.

ISBN 13 : 978-0-9560645-4-7

Printed and bound by CPI Group (UK) Ltd, Croydon, CR0 4YY

Check out Spoz's website at ... **www.spoz.co**

U.K. £11.99 RRP (complete with CD)

Acknowledgements

Some of the poems in this book have popped up in an assortment of other places, before appearing on these pages. It's tough keeping track, and frankly, I haven't done a great job of keeping track, so don't be surprised if you see them popping up in an assortment of other places.

Having said that, I do know that *The Castle Up the Beacon* was commissioned by the BBC for National Poetry Day 2016. Nice one BBC ... much appreciated. It also appears in *Spoz's Shorts ... and the Occasional Long One.*

I've also lost count of the numbers of websites (as well as which ones) that have displayed some of these poems, as film or audio, within their virtual pages. Thank you ... all of you.

There's an accompanying CD in the back of this book. If there isn't ... then you've been careless and lost it ... or robbed.

The contents list in this book is the same as the running order of the CD. All musician and composer credits are listed in the back of this book.

FOR MOM

CONTENTS

Picture of Spoz by Bohdan Piasecki

Fun

**The night is young and so are you,
You've already necked a few,
But, like a kiddy in *Cadbury World*,
You gaze upon a rainbow of delights
and realise ... it's going to be one of
those nights.**

**An unattainable cleavage, cleaves the
money from your pocket,
For that kaleidoscope of clever juice
that fires your rocket,
Don't knock it ...
It's blue, it's pink, it's green, it's clear,
it's anyone of these,
It tastes like "Covonia" cough linctus
and looks like anti-freeze,
It's cheap at twice the price, you can
never pay too much,
For the courage it bestows ... albeit
Dutch.**

**So you neck a few ... three more than
two**

And you're good ... tall as a tower,
Your excess is the access to your own corridor of power.
Like the Don, you're full of offers no one can refuse,
You can't lose.
Driven by the booze you spot a girl,
Wearing so little she could get arrested,
Give her some chat,
But she ain't interested,
She wants a higher return on what she's invested and it ain't you ...
No where near ...
So have another beer and a vodka shot,
"I'll come back later when you're hot to trot ..."
What?
Do people still say that?
No, it's just the vodka talking,
And it's calling you a twat.

So you neck a few more ... one less than four and you're good ...
Hard as nails,

You're in a town that never fails to
deliver jailbirds for jails,
'Cause you're a dick by day so why be
different in the dark?
You're about to become a dog who's
bite's worse than his bark.

Oh look ...
It's that girl again ... the one with next to
nothing on from 'Next'
And you're vexed ... and ...
"Who's that wanker she's with?
Look at the way he talks!"
Your fuse is lit ...
You're Guy Fawkes ...
You're fit to burst ...
He's James the First ...

Then, before you know it,
You've blown it,
The first punch lands twelve hours after
you've thrown it.
In with another ... he stalls,
In with the boot ... he falls,

Down comes the mist, the time bomb's ticking,
His eyes roll, he goes limp but you don't stop kicking.

You see ... one's notion of fun can vary a lot,
What makes something funny and what makes it ... not,
Getting pissed with your mates may be a source of hilarity,
But at what point does "fun" turn into vulgarity?
It lacks clarity ... it's vague,
By whose rule do we measure?
Are all acts of fun designed to give pleasure?
A moment to treasure,
Or a moment of greed,
When self satisfaction,
Surpasses your need.

Beaumont
Beaumont

HARVIESTOUN
2 1 3
SUMMER LEGEND
EASY IPA
INDEPENDENTLY INSPECTED
CASK MARQUE
Cellar Cool
CASK MARQUE
Cellar Cool
3.55

ASBO Kid

As I listen to the radio spouting a 'lock
'em up' mentality,
The right wing reality dawns,
With streams of words and no thoughts
in the pauses.
Condemning the effects,
Though never questioning the causes.
So in a fit of frustration,
I phoned up the radio station,
To offer my words of measured
moderation.

Yeah ... right.

Words that were meant with the best
intent,
Though seemed to fall ... lost on the
ground ...
So I turned up my volume ...
but still no sound,
As my words were met by walls of
ignorance,
So my face folded and frowned.

Now, I know facial expressions don't really work on radio,
But were my words getting through?
In hindsight .... maybe no.
'Cause all I got was short shrift from the presenter's moanin'
And he was only really qualified to do a 'football phone in'.
Didn't realise that to question the wherefores and whys,
Is not to justify ... not the same as condoning.
And there he was ... prescribing cures and pouring scorn,
On conditions that had been left to fester since ... well ... before I was born.

So, fed up of listening to his incessant shite,
I wound up my words and bid him goodnight.

That's when it happened ...
All those words that, while I was on air,

I wanted to say,
Turned up when I hung up ...
Ain't it always the way?

Words that differentiate between
disenfranchised and delinquent,
Distinguish between unable and
unwilling ... it's chilling,
As the social mincing machine keeps
churning and churning,
Turning lost hope into an unreasonable
yearning,
For what society and the media tells
them "You must have!",
Or Murdoch's scummy empire will label
you a chav and a loser,
Consumerism is their drug and they're
making you the user,
Though never fully fulfilling what a
balanced diet is really all about ...
Because shit in ...
Usually equals shit out.

So ... the lost boy loots and the lost girl
screams,

As they clutch and cradle their dying dreams that are drowning ...
Drowning faster...
Faster than the last witch that was thrown into the cut
Of the last apathetic disaster.

He stands in the doorway of despair, knowing he's going to go in,
As the bouncer looks him up and down
And grins another knowing grin.
He's choking on the right wing rhetoric and vomit,
That yesterday's *Daily Mail* front page had splattered on it.
Quick to judge, quick to anger, quick to reprimand,
Slow to understand.
Corner any animal and it'll always bite your hand,
'Cause that's what he does
And it's what his dad and his dad's dad did:
They're only the dead dreams of the ASBO kid.

And then tomorrow, in class, if he gets that far,
The cycle starts again:
The cycle of mental pain;
The cycle of bad name;
The cycle of shame;
The cycle that can only end when the chain breaks and the brakes make the wheels stop turning and start the learning.
Because the next steps might be the ones of no return to pastures greener ...
Or at least to some pastures with some grass on,
With hopes and dreams to pass on ...
Of pavements with no broken glass on
And who knows ...
Even a cup of tea and a croissant,
That's been bought and paid for from a local independent retailer,
Rather than a corporate franchise,
Seek the truth ... don't laud the lies,
Let's do up the laces of what a failed legacy undid,
One less dead dream -
One less ASBO kid.

TDH

Letter to Birmingham

Dear Birmingham,

Somewhere between pre pubescent
intoxication and the Broad Street slags
that became the new generation of
mothers and fathers,
A blurred family of be-cycled helmets
Are unfazed by the fenced off funfair that
fun forgot.

So they just kept going,
Never really knowing whether this was
just another act
Of wanton neglect that they had grown
to expect,
Or whether, Birmingham, like so many
other things ...
You were going to get round to it ...
sometime ... soon ... honest.

You see Birmingham,
You hadn't put any money in the meter
for months,

Turning it in to a health and safety hazard,
Sodden in winter, awaiting the blizzard.
And somewhere in your Birmingham air,
A Morrissey melody made its way down from Manchester.
Not everyday is like Sunday everywhere,
But today, in this and a few more corners of the city ... it was.

Racing cars had been impounded,
Spaceships and rockets were grounded
And the novelty merry-go-round sounded sorry for itself,
As it drowned in its unrelenting hushes,
No laughing ... no playing ...
No adrenalin rushes.

But there were blue skies once Birmingham,
As blue as a Saturday afternoon at St. Andrews,
And win or lose you're still free to choose the avenues that lead to our sunshine within ...

Cue cello strings and violins, ELO's and Jeff Lynnes,
One love ends as another begins
And your sins are forgiven, your slate wiped clean,
Short memories forget where you had once been.

And you *have* been in love Birmingham, I know you have,
Because you've seen the stars reflect in your reservoirs,
But you've also seen new born calves
Slaughtered in your abattoirs,
Been a bystander and stood by on faux pas,
Crashed into parked cars and walked away from the scene,
Neglecting to wipe your arse coming out of the latrine...
... you daft bastard.

Birmingham, we're splayed out resplendent on your bed,
Like a party frock on prom night,

Waiting for you to grab our love handles
And rodger us to within an inch of our lives.
But sometimes ... you're as limp as a lettuce in a desert,
As flaccid as a ninety year old stoner on acid, drunk on gin,
Sometimes, you just can't thumb it in.
Sometimes, you babble like a brook
When you could rage like a river,
Sometimes, you're like a dodgy UPS truck: you just don't deliver.

But Birmingham, I will always continue to give you my all.
Every mess of excess and thoughtless shortfall,
You've been maimed and mauled but remain immortal,
The welcome mat at the door for every beck and call.
There was always room at your Inn for my dad and mum,
Yes Brum, it didn't matter where they came from,

You shot and bombed them in one decade,
Then helped them out in the next one.

You've been butchered by the country, heckled and harassed,
Broken tools and triple heart bypassed,
Forced to be the underclass
Just because of the way you speak
And you know it's bleak,
when elocution electrocution treatment is a must,
Or be defined by your accent ...
Shit or bust.

But I trust you Birmingham.
I trust your half cut grins and gin soaked whims
That swim like breeze blocks in Speedos,
But we know you've been short changed, slightly deranged
And never fully fulfilled your function,
They interchanged you ...
Like spaghetti junction ...
Them bastards.

adidas

Shiny,
Shitty,
Shoddy,
"Cum on feel the noise" said Noddy.
Dodgy scores and Ozzy Osbourne's roars,
Pouring scorn aboard profanity's shoulders,
But nobody told us you were catching boulders fired from Tolkien's catapults,
Where far canals get closer on aqueducts.

Shires were born on your hills and mills,
Giving birth to middle earth,
You read the books of countless towers and crystal palaces,
Took gulps from poisoned chalices and flaccid fallacies,
Handed down by the lying limbs of bastards' calluses,
You really know what malice is,
But I still can't resist yer...
You're slightly taboo,
Like my best friend's sister.

Birmingham, don't listen when them bastards start dissin'
'Cause I love you more with three or four marbles missing.
They tell me you have lied, but I don't believe a word,
As town council after town council
Polishes and paints turds
Before shitting out new ones,
And a million Gary Newbons will laugh at the sport
Of a hundred councillors that have sold you short ... them bastards.

And they used to say you were a city of a thousand trades,
Most of which are now "streamlined" or "out sourced",
Forced out by bean counters and gaffers who were paid off,
Then let off like Barabbas,
Leaving you and your people with the abacus
to count the real cost,

And for every skill and resource lost and tossed into landfill,
You, our Mother of Invention will give birth to ten more:
Some may be still born,
Some are feral yet fragile,
Some are live and kicking,
Frantically flipping the bird
to all who say ...
"But aren't you from *that* City?"

Yes I fucking am, you bastards.

I'm of you and from you Birmingham
And I'll keep hitting them as long as you keep serving them,
Swerving them balls around walls beyond keepers' reaches,
'Till our features are rich,
Like the suns of beaches.

Beautiful Brum, keep cocking a deaf 'un,
To them bastards who say you need teaching a lesson.

They get thrills to instil you with fear and distress an'
They're just cold meat;
You're the delicatessen.

So Birmingham, when them bastards try to tell you
That you're the dog shit stuck on their shoe,
Tell them that you won't wash off,
Tell them you're the trash can full of untold gems,
Tell them you're the dandelion flower amidst their bouquet stems,
Tell them you'll keep getting up
After every punch in the guts or kick to the nuts,
Tell them that you just don't give a fuck.

Laughing with your yellowed teeth,
Laughing like the bullied boy
Who stands up high when bullets fly,
'Cause he's way past caring ...

Laughing like the mad beggar who has two tenths of fuck all, yet still insists on sharing.

Laughing long,
Laughing loud,
Laughing proud ...

At them bastards.

The Castle Up the Beacon

I can see your house from here ...
In fact, I can see *all* of your houses from here.
And when the weather's clear
And the sky's as blue as a Saturday afternoon at St. Andrew's,
Win or lose, I will always choose ...

This.

I'm your borderland beacon that bore down on you from birth,
Giving Rubery a view like 'Google Earth'
Before you even knew what computers were.

They call me a 'toposcope' these days,
But I will always be your castle ...
More than just a Cadbury treat
sat upon this grassy hill,
And from this toppest top
It's hard to see,

The veins of your rich realities,
Your variety of societies and your diverse nationalities.

Zoomed out up here hides the hustle and hurry of you,
Webbed feet flapping like the clappers,
When all I see is a swan ...
But I know what goes on.

I've felt it in the happy skips of inner city children,
I've heard it in the banter of a hundred different languages,
I've smelt it in a thousand trades
Of glass and cars and chocolate,
I've sampled it in spices,
Samosas and cheese sandwiches.

I've been watching Birmingham
And The Black Country grow, up here,
I can see roads like rivers,
Ebb and flow, up here,
I've wept with family generations as they come and go, up here,

I've seen the fervent kisses
of mistletoe, up here.

I've chuckled at tangled kite strings and
clumsy gamboles,
Laughed at pet dog picnic pirates as they
plundered ham roles,
I'm the fortress in the forest,
That you long to get lost in,
I'm the smile on your face ...
I am ace ...
I am bostin.

Endangered Species

We're an endangered species,
Wading through faeces and bent on oblivion.
Craving half chances, but nobody's giving them.
'Cause we've got our own lives and we're just too busy living them,
To be stopping and thinking
About those on the brink and seeing they're our neighbours.

We're gorging ourselves on the fruits of our labours,
Or as is often the case,
Someone else's ...
A twisted notion of what real wealth is.

Because some people judge well being by the balance on a bank sheet,
And sure,
We all want to live and eat comfortably,
But be honest with me ...

Who the fuck needs a Range Rover in London?

Unless you're taking it "up the heath" in Hampstead like George Michael,
'Cause 4X4 is better by far than any car or motor cycle.

Trade in your Bentley,
Part ex your Aston Martin,
If it's a fight you're after then you better stop starting,
Because what you call a necessity
Is like a red rag to a bull to me.
These baubles and trinkets are a vulgar obscenity,
They're like a profanity,
That adequately displays your lack of humanity,
It's just vanity ... and it ain't fair.

While your cup runneth over with hundreds,
There are thousands and millions who don't even have cups,

There's something missing,
There's no pot to piss in,
Can you unblock your ears 'cause you ain't even listening!

A generation tainted by a media's "dissing".

Disenfranchised
Dismembered
Discriminated
Disremembered

There are whole communities of poor sods conned,
Who keep the relative minorities in all mod - cons,
Their muted cries are louder than bombs,
As they fall on deaf eyes and blind ears.
The fat end of the wedge ain't been this fat in years,
A society so senseless and desensitised these days,
It makes me want to ...
Mix up my clichés.

But what's that self righteous quip I hear you say?
About paying the taxes you're asked to pay,
About earning and spending the way that you choose,
About how exploitation's just another tool to use,
About working hard, playing hard, every day,
About stepping on fingers to make your way,
About the feckless reaping their just rewards,
But when I tell you that your reasoning's flawed,
You come back with your usual contented retort...

"You're just jealous mate".

RANG

£10800
£10350
£8050
£8050
£6750
£14500
£10200
ROLEX

Football for Palestine

Months of Sundays have passed us by,
Yet all I see is now.
Where Palestine only drinks
When the Israeli authorities allow,
Because wars are waged by withholding water,
So that livelihoods and livestock,
Face the drawn out slaughter of thirst,
Where bouts of manufactured droughts
leave a land once blessed ...
Now cursed.

Cursed by the daylight robbery,
That runs rampant from the river to the sea,
Cursed by the scorched earth
Of a flash grenade and tear gas spree,
Cursed by a torn out and replanted olive tree
That claims a tortured truth,
Yet a multitude of broken cameras
Are inadmissible as proof.

I see makeshift umbrellas against a hard rain,
That showers market stalls with debris and disdain,
Rocks and rubbish again and again,
Under the IDF's watchful eyes.
Yet they're deaf, dumb and blind to the cries of victims they're told and have grown to despise,
Hunger strikers facing death,
All because of their love of life ...
A bitter, twisted irony,
In the homeland of the Christ.

So we play the beautiful game with beautiful people,
Who face anxiety and upheaval from illegal settlements built on stolen land,
Where a call for justice will bring down the heavy hand of an apartheid state,
That tries to silence cries of freedom,
That persist and resist ...
And refuse to capitulate.

So,

For a short while we raise a smile and reconcile,
That whilst our actions may appear small,
Our solidarity is shared with the kick of a ball,
Our words on the walls that we'd gladly trade for bridges,
Are words for humanity that go beyond religious.
Hold onto your wishes, your dreams, your defiance,
Like the words in the anthem of
The Small Heath Alliance,
Existence is resistance,
Let's share the load ...
And keep right on
To the end
Of the road.

DS
WWJD

Losing It

**For thirty five years he was that man.
That man who'd get up some time after
six and take his biggest risk ...
Cornflakes or Weetabix?**

**That man who fell out of bed and fell into
work.
And though, sometimes,
It would drive him berserk,
He drove his Ford into a car park full of
Beamers and Mercs.
Offices full of suited jerks
With hands up skirts
Of the junior clerks,
His head full of failure ...
It would often hurt.**

**His wife had long ... since ... gone.
Found someone whose head wasn't
screwed on so tight,
Took her out at night just so they could
spend time together:**

The guy wasn't big or clever,
He was just ... there.
He cared.
He broke up her monotony with his verve and spontaneity,
Cradled her in his bassinet arms in her moments of frailty,
He saw so many things her husband had failed to see.

The kids had grown and flown the nest,
The best part of two years previous
To his wife discovering her new found genius.
It was like her purpose for staying had gone when the kids had,
And her life had turned a bit sad,
Since the spark had died for her kids' dad.
Which, in all honesty, had happened years before the kids left.
He was a moron marooned and a beggar bereft.
His pallet of music had been treble cleft beyond repair.

And all he could do was stare ...
And watch her ship sail ...
And feel his life fail ... as his cabin became water logged ...
And his days became groundhogged.

But today ... was going to be different.

All this time he'd been doing a job that he thought was a career,
And it was blatantly clear,
That he was never going to get there ... from here.
Here ... where nobody's shit smelled,
Here ... where his surname was always fucking mis-spelled,
Here ... where loyalty and service are just pissed on,
Here ... where you can't smell a rat,
Until you've kissed one.

Some said they should have seen it coming,
Some said it was no surprise,

Others tried to demonise
When they realised,
Their ignorance and lack of compassion
May have nurtured the worm that turned on the corpses that fed it,
May have written the pages of the book, that blew up in the hands of those that read it.

Nobody saw the light at the end of his tunnel go out,
Nor ask what his silent tears were all about,
Nobody saw him burst into flame,
In the same way that nobody took the time to learn, or call him by, his first name.

And nobody forgot what he did that day,
And nobody would remain unscathed,
And the blame was tossed and the buck was passed,
And the rueful shuffled ...
Whenever questions were asked.

SCREAMING
INTERNALLY
ExtraCare
PARKING TICKET

<u>Are We Nearly There Yet?</u>

There are always the days
We will want to forget ...
... but will sadly remember.
Sliding scales on a downward trend,
From Octobers to Novembers
And round the bend to groundhogged
Yule logs and ...
"We never knew there'd be nothing new",
New Years.

A million resolutions
in lieu of a revolution,
That may or may not be televised,
Yet needs to be realised,
So we can claim the real prize,
Of a righteous constitution,
Get wise and reject the compromised
refrain,
That you can expect to hear again and
again ...
Turn and face the strain ...
Ch ... ch ... changes
Are what we need,

To ensure it's more than just the chosen few ... who succeed.
Because the criteria for choice is skewed
And when you allude to wealth being a measure of achievement,
I can see common sense has suffered a bereavement.
And while you may be vehement
In your disagreement,
I will take your opinions on board;
Like a ship's captain takes on board infected rats,
Yeah ... call me a bigot,
You fucking fat cats,
Getting morbidly obese as you feed us scraps,
Diverting world attention with fabricated facts.
You know a few bullshit brass tacks
Will get the wide eyed plebs and proles,
Behaving and berating like arseholes.
"It's the immigrants, it's the Poles,
It's no border controls,
That will bring England the brave to her knees ...

It's asylum seekers, it's refugees!"
As they digest a diet
Of right wing nob cheese.

Millions stare salivating as privileged classes gorge their arses,
Suckling on an unsustainably swollen breast,
Mother knows best but is repeatedly raped by the beast ...
The one percent,
Triggering a winter of discontent that will last for all seasons,
Where the pursuit of peace is labelled treason ...
And if money is not your God,
You're considered a heathen.

This well established establishment of yours,
Continually skips through revolving doors of plenty,
While our continuous chores leave our bellies empty.
Is that how it's meant to be?

Sphere
is here.

You're busy manipulating the subjectivity
Of fairness and equality,
Blatantly dragging out your career's longevity,
Spitting on morality and your personal integrity,
If you ever had any.
You move the goalposts so often these days,
You've put them on castors,
Anxious dancers for your puppet masters,
Attention diverters from displeasing disasters,
"So sorry we killed and maimed and hurt yer, but you got in the way of our 'cash converter'!"

I face palm myself so much these days, my cheek's gone red,
Tossing and turning in bed,
While I figuratively *and* literally
pull hair from my head,
Common senses dead or too close to death,

Even my scrabble tiles keep coming up with "WTF".

So as we drive down the road toward equity,
Through the wind and the rain and the snow and the kids ask,
"Are we nearly there yet, dad?"
"Well kids ... we've a long way to go".

Valentine's Day in the Jungle

I hear stories.

Stories of a sinking ship that can carry no more.
Can't make it ashore 'cause it's packed to the brim;
Where conditions are poor and pickings are slim.
It sounds grim ...
But while sailors squabble
Over scraps and squeezed spaces,
The opulent officers wear grins on their faces,
As they drill holes of austerity in the hull,
Whilst reciting their well rehearsed mantra ... "the ship is full".
Yet, they swing fat cats and gorge in their enormous quarters,
Building barbed wire barriers,
Instead of bridges over waters ...
Exporters of war and slaughter to order,
With a barrage of broad sides
on a biased border.

I see stories.

I see stories of hope and resilience,
Where others are told to see fear and ambivalence,
The threat of disobedience and an assault on sensibilities...
Just pathetic excuses for continued hostilities.
I see frozen faces with the warmest smiles,
Where others are told to see rapists and paedophiles.
I see the cost of ignorance and neglect,
People paying high prices,
Where others are told to see terrorists,
Told to devour divisive devices ...
So why alarms and why surprises,
When a doorstep challenge
becomes a crisis?
I see families who have cried so many tears, they have none left.
One time blessed though now bereft
On Calais' coastline as unwelcome guests.

Live
As Brothers
or Die
as fools
NO WAR
we need you
NANOU

So how apt and fitting it is,
That those benevolent French authorities
See refugees with tearless eyes,
Blood shot and raw,
So provide them with canisters
filled with more.

I tell stories.

I tell stories ‘till I’m hoarse,
But is anyone listening?
Compassion’s gone missing and right
wing rhetoric resolve is stiffening.
It’s as crippling as Annie Wilkes in
‘Misery’,
Yet Joseph marches on
In the midst of this artillery.
He’s here because he’s sure
metaphors won’t kill
As quickly as the civil war in
West Sudan will.
This once proud man tells me of his plight
in ‘Pidgin English’,
It’s left him morally molested
and pigeon chested,

**Says he'll swim the channel if he has to,
once he's fully rested from his last
attempt at stowing away ...
So we drink tea together ...
On Valentine's Day.**

**And I make no apology
And I refuse to say sorry, when I say,
"The best thing to come out of France?
Right now?
Would be a thousand hopeful smiles
on the back of a lorry,
A humane quarry and a ferry full of hope,
not hate, to fill our soul,
With an open gate ... at border control."
Because these are the sad and selfish
days
Where we need to over-stand
open gates work both ways ...
There's a whole globe waiting
for the xenophobe,
Good riddance to bad rubbish please!
Because I can't think of a fairer trade,
Than fascists for refugees.**

My Heritage ... Innit?

To resemble someone of stature,
Or to capture a feature that rouses rapture,
Could be classed as a wonderful thing...
Perhaps you're the image of
Martin Luther King?
Or perhaps Ghandi, John Lennon, Kate Bush or Bob Marley ...
Me? I look a bit like the great ...
Joe Pasquale.
But that's okay, 'cause he's a nice guy,
So don't try and belittle me,
Because both Joe and I have an affinity with Italy.

And I've been there.

That speck of an Italian village where mom and dad came from,
Like that nugget from heaven,
And I'm wondering if it's the same one
That they left behind. Jeeze ...
Were mom and dad blind?

Though I guess things are never quite what they seem,
'Cause it's a bitch being the cat that never gets the cream.

So ... it's "Arividerci Campania" and "Buon giorno ... Brum!"
I'm so glad that Mom and Dad
had decided to come to the UK,
To start a new life in a new way,
'Cause if they'd have decided to stay,
I could have been herding goats now,
With my farming know how, that I would have acquired,
Had their work permits expired,
Or they'd chosen *not* to be part of that labour migration,
That made my mom and dad
foreigners in this nation.

And didn't they know it.

So it's "Hi ho, hi ho"
It's off to work they go,
Treat him hard, he's a wop,

Treat her rough, she's a dago.
It's tough trying to work *and* pick up a language,
When all you want is-a 'panini',
To make-a da sandwich.

Then, us kids come along
And it's school days anew,
The Catholic nuns changed our names,
'Cause "Giovanni won't do! We'll call you John, it's much easier to say, it's what the English translation is, anyway.
You can call him what you like when you're in your own home,
But as you eye-talians say ...
'When in Rome'...".

Now ... don't shed a tear,
Don't pass round the tissues,
'Cause I'm wondering if Joe Pasquale had to face the same issues of 'funny name' taunts in his neighbourhood,
Thanks to Enoch Powell and his rivers of blood.

**Anyway ... Giovanni fades,
But John works hard in class,
Heads down and study and I hope that I
pass my exams.**

**So what were Mom and Dad's plans?
Well, they didn't want me following in
their tracks ...
Long hours, hard labour, sweating blood,
breaking their backs.
"Wek with-a you brain, (this'll be my mom
talking by the way) ... getta good pay
anna sev a bita money for da rainy day,
Get-a nice-a house anna get-a nice car
Anna don west-a too much-a time with-a
play da guitar"**

**So that's *nearly* what I did and that's
really why I'm here,
To pay homage to two stalwarts and all,
I hold dear.
The definition of the axis upon which I
revolve,
Is down to their courage, their strength
and resolve.**

CD CONTENTS & CREDITS

1. FUN

Words by Spoz. Music by Loz Rabone
Beats, loops, guitar, programming and production by Loz too.

2. ASBO KID

Words by Spoz. Music by Zack Esposito
Beats, loops, programming and production by Zack too.

3. LETTER TO BIRMINGHAM

Words by Spoz. Music by Tim Balnaves
Beats, loops, piano, programming and production by Tim too.

4. CASTLE UP THE BEACON

Words by Spoz. Music by Loz Rabone
Beats, loops, programming and production by Loz too. Piano played by Tim Balnaves.

5. ENDANGERED SPECIES

Words by Spoz. Music by Loz Rabone
Beats, loops, programming and production by Loz too.

6. FOOTBALL FOR PALESTINE

Words by Spoz. Music by Zack Esposito
Beats, loops, programming and production by Zack too.

7. LOSING IT

Words by Spoz. Music by Loz Rabone
Beats, loops, guitar, programming and production by Loz too.

8. ARE WE NEARLY THERE YET?

Words by Spoz. Music by Spoz and Zack Esposito. Beats, loops, programming and production by Zack too. Spoz played guitar.

9. VALENTINE'S DAY IN THE JUNGLE

Words by Spoz. Music by Spoz and Loz Rabone. Beats, loops, programming and production by Loz too. Spoz played guitar.

10. MI HERITAGE INNIT?

Words by Spoz. Music by Loz Rabone
Clarinet played by Tom Martin
Production by Loz.

This is a list of people who have inspired me, influenced me or helped me in anyway (whether they know it or not). So allow me to say "thank you".

Mama e Papa e la famiglia Esposito
Zack, Fran and Claude xxx
Dreadlockalien, Elvis McGonagall, Bowie, AF Harrold, John Hegley, John Cooper Clarke, Attila the Stockbroker, Hollie McNish, Steve Pottinger, Kate Tempest, Polar Bear, Rob Gee, Berko, Andy Craven Griffiths, Longfella, Vaseline, Skabucks, Ben Folds, Johnny Fluffypunk, Jess Green, Keiron King, The Antipoet, Pete the Temp, Jodi Anne Bickley, Hannah Teasdale, Bohdan Piasecki, Leon Priestnall, Matt Windle, Holly Daffurn, The brilliant Ten Letters crew, namely Lorna, Aliyah H, Aliyah D, Callum, Melissa, Maggie, Nyanda, Jasmine, Carl, Sipho, Luci, Casey, Emma, Cookie, Hannah, Zack and Stringy P (and Jord!). Every one in the Brum poetry scene, especially Amerah, Kamil, Lexi, Hayley, Tom McC, Sean Colletti, Jimmy and Big Bren.

**Poetry on Loan (nice one Brenda!),
Birmingham, Worcestershire, Shropshire
and Staffordshire Libraries,
Steve Wilson and Worcestershire Arts,
Jonathan and Writing West Midlands,
Arts Council West Midlands (cheers James!)
Marcus and Sara-Jane,
Apples and Snakes especially Jacob and
Lisa (and the rest of you obviously!),
Birmingham Youth Service,
Women and Theatre,
Anisa and the Beatfreeks crew,
Olly and everyone at NAF,
The Palace Theatre in Redditch,
Artrix Theatre in Bromsgrove,
MAC Birmingham,
Siobhan Tyrie (thanks bab!),
All the schools I've visited and yet to visit,
especially the teachers and staff who have
been brilliantly supportive under stress and
all the kids who have been ace, even though
they thought (and probably still think)
"poetry's boring".**

...and anyone else who knows me.

Picture of Spoz by John Davenport

A Bit About the Author

SPOZ ... was born in Rubery, which is on the South Birmingham / North Worcestershire border. His real name is Giovanni Esposito. 'Spoz' comes from his surname ... the bit between the 'E' and the 'ito' (sort of).

SPOZ ... was Birmingham's Poet Laureate in 2006 / 7 (which was nice) and is resident poet at Birmingham City Football Club (not so nice sometimes, but ... KRO!)

SPOZ ... is a poetry and 'poetry slam' workshop facilitator in primary and secondary schools all over the world.

SPOZ ... looks a bit like Joe Pasquale.

SPOZ ... can be contacted via his website www.spoz.co

Spoz has written two other poetry books suitable for children (none of the sweary nonsense that's contained in this one). The titles are ...

The Day the Earth Grew Hair ... and other stuff **(Bostin Publications)**

Spoz's Shorts ... and the Occasional Long One **(Caboodle Books)**

Both are available via his website ...

www.spoz.co